CW01080602

Healing Emotional Wounds

Other "Spiritual Companions"

Healing Emotional Wounds

by Robert R. Leichtman, M.D.
& Carl Japikse

ENTHEA PRESS
Atlanta, Georgia

HEALING EMOTIONAL WOUNDS
Copyright © 1979 by Light

All Rights Reserved. No part of this book
may be used or reproduced in any manner
without written permission, except in the
case of brief quotations embodied in ar-
ticles and reviews. Printed in the United
States of America. Direct inquiries to:
Enthea Press, P.O. Box 297, Marble Hill,
GA 30148

ISBN 0-89804-829-X

Introduction

These essays on *Healing Emotional Wounds* were first published as part of a set of 30 essays written by Robert R. Leichtman, M.D. and Carl Japikse on *The Art of Living*. They can also be found in Volume II of that series.

Healing Emotional Wounds has been selected to be reprinted in this special gift edition because these essays have helped many people put their shattered emotions back together again.

In her introduction to Volume II of *The Art of Living*, Olga Worrall writes: "These essays contain thought-provoking ideas that will stimulate our thinking and help us in our endeavors to create a better life."

The first essay deals with the nature of the emotions; the second with the importance of forgiving others—and life.

For information about ordering other essays by Dr. Leichtman and Mr. Japikse, please turn to page 136.

The Nature
& Purpose
of the Emotions

A Lack of Understanding

The nature and purpose of any thing is seldom apparent without careful observation and intuitive comprehension. Even a simple object such as a tea pot would be enough to baffle a person who did not already know what it was—from being told or by observing it in use. To be sure, if the individual spent enough time analyzing the pot, he would probably draw some correct conclusions about its nature, such as the fact that the spout can be used to pour. But other details would go unnoticed, and when it came to determining the purpose of the object, he would undoubtedly misinterpret it entirely. For example, observing the designs on the outside of the pot, he might conclude that its purpose is only for display. Or, noting the large opening in the top, he might decide that it is a container for storing paper clips or pennies. Indeed, the chances are remote that he would ever, by himself, conclude that this object's purpose is for brewing and serving tea.

There are many aspects of life that the average person among us has studied no more completely than our hypothetical friend has examined his teapot. As a result, we go through life believing in false notions and trying to live up to them—an unrealistic proposition. Not understanding the nature of these aspects of life, we find it very difficult to control them. Not comprehending their purpose, we end up using them in ways for which they were never intended—and rarely in the ways for which they were designed.

The most notable example of this misuse of our human equipment is in the realm of emotions. Very few of us have ever spent the time to carefully examine the characteristics of our emotions, and even fewer have intuitively speculated

upon—and learned—the purpose of emotions. Instead, the majority of us are well
satisfied to try to use our emotions on the
basis of mistaken observations, erroneous
conclusions, and illusory opinions. We
have gathered some facts: we know that
emotions are important, we know that
they can cause psychological pain to our-
selves and to others, and we know that they
can also give pleasure. But we have failed
to make many relevant observations. Most
of us, for example, cannot even distinguish between emotions and thoughts and
frequently try to use them interchangeably. Furthermore, we have erred in our
conclusions regarding the purpose of
emotions: we are often misled by the outer
appearances of feelings and conclude that
their purpose is to be entertaining, gratify-
ing, or self-stimulating. Or, we become
hypnotized by the power of our desires
and decide that our emotions are to be
containers for storing small items: petty
wants, grudges and resentments, vanities,
a bit of pride, and other baubles. Each of
these common notions about emotions is

a direct opposite of the genuine purpose of human emotions.

In the hands of someone who does not know what it is, a teapot has little significance. In the hands of someone who understands its nature and purpose, however, a teapot can be most useful. The same could be said about our emotions—although of course they are far more important to us than a teapot. Moreover, like a china teapot, they are very fragile and can easily be shattered when used incorrectly and unwisely. It is not hard to imagine our hypothetical friend's investigation of the pot ending in disaster: in trying to discover how strong the pot was, for example, he might easily subject it to too much pressure and crack it. Unfortunately, we often treat our emotions in much the same fashion. After a little unwise experimentation in the experiences of living, our emotions lie in shards about us, cutting and jabbing whoever might venture close. We make an effort to pick up the pieces and glue them back together again, but usually are not very successful. Why not? *Because we fail to understand the nature and purpose of our emotions.* We have no fundamental pattern from which to work.

This lack of understanding is a serious problem. For most of us, our emotions are the dominant focus of our consciousness—we operate through our emotions far more than through any other aspect of the personality. We have a physical consciousness and a mental consciousness as well as an emotional consciousness, but the vast majority of us use the feeling side of our humanity as the primary mode of both perception and expression. (This is not the most desirable condition, to be sure, but at this point in human evolution, it is the norm—a norm that will continue as such for a long time to come.) Consequently, learning to comprehend the nature and purpose of our emotions is no trivial matter. It can free us from many of our problems. It can make us more efficient individuals, better able to achieve our goals. It can help us to relate more fully and more lovingly to the other people in our lives. It can help us participate more completely in the purposes of the universe as a whole.

Most of us are emotional beings. Our lives are almost wholly made up of emotional events and conditions. We are so accustomed to thinking emotionally and reacting emotionally that the other aspects of our being—our common sense, for example—are often overshadowed and controlled by our emotions. As a result, if something happens to powerfully disturb the emotions—with fear, anger, grief, or anything else—most of us become paralyzed on all levels of being. Fear is a dramatic case in point. Its effect on the average person is well known. The mind stops working and the body freezes, unable to move or act. Panic ensues. Many disasters resulting in death can be attributed to one tragic condition: the individuals involved are paralyzed by panic—the emotion of fear.

Why are the emotions such a dominating factor in the lives of most of us? The answer to this question has to do with environment. Why do people from the southeastern portions of the United States speak with a drawl, operate at a more leisurely pace, and have somewhat different customs than people from Chicago or New York? Because their environment has conditioned them to speak and act in those ways. The southerner has grown up in one environment and the northerner in a slightly different one, and so there are differences in their respective lifestyles.

Psychologically, our emotions form the primary environment that most of us dwell in. A few people live in a primarily mental environment (and even fewer live in a truly spiritual environment), but the overwhelming majority of us live almost exclusively in an emotional environment: an atmosphere of happiness, sadness, anger, affection, calmness, hate, despair, peace, jealousy, acceptance, embarrassment, forgiveness, and so on. We are raised in the midst of this environment, we accept it as natural, and most of us continue to live in it throughout the years of our lives. This is not a private environment; it encompasses the entire Planet and affects all of us equally, until we learn the nature and purpose of our emotions and thus learn to control them. And the content of this planetary emotional environment influences our individual lives just as much as (actually, more than) the conditions of our physical environment shape and mold us.

Every emotion that washes upon us from our environment has its impact upon us. If we are in tune with intense negativity and stress at work or home, we are subconsciously influenced by that negativity—for the worse. If we are in tune with friendliness, joy, and peace, we are subtly affected by these beneficent feelings—for the better. Conversely, every emotion that we, as an individual, feel or express has an impact upon the environment around us. Our sadness tends to infect others and make them sad. Our good cheer is likewise contagious and tends to lighten the moods and burdens of others.

This interplay between ourself and our emotional environment is a constant process and determines, to a large degree, our basic moods, attitudes, and behavior. Because of its importance, it is something that each of us should carefully study—to see how and why this emotional environment operates, and how we each fit into it. And as a consequence of this study, we should each review our basic intent in using our emotions, revising them so they express the best within us.

Toward this end, this essay will examine closely the nature of our emotions—their properties, their characteristics, their activities, and how to control them. It will also consider the purpose of emotions and point out common misconceptions. The underlying theme throughout will be *developing an increasingly enlightened intent in using emotions.*

The proper use of emotions is vital to our well-being, our personal achievement, and our growth. It is a prerequisite for becoming a master in the art of living. Our emotions are modes of expression that can either help or hinder us—depending on how we use them. Properly used, they can express the best within us: the roots of our humanity, love, joy, and goodwill. Improperly handled, they can betray the worst within us: malice, envy, hostility, selfishness, pettiness, pride, and intolerance. We can use our emotions to nurture wonderful qualities and ideals within other people, and thus help them grow and evolve. Or, we can use our emotions to destroy the goodness within ourself and others—a blight that kills life and smothers opportunity.

Thus, the manner in which we use our emotions depends not only on our understanding of them, but also on our intent. Understanding their nature can help us correct careless misuses of our emotional energies. But only dedication to the unselfish purposes of the Universal Life can prevent misuses caused by irresponsible intention.

Living Streams of Energy

In examining the nature of emotions, it is wise to start by considering what they are not. Emotions are not physical energy or even physical sensation, even though they sometimes seem to be. Who has not felt a surge of blood in the face at moments of embarrassment, a shiver of nervous energy up the spine at moments of excitement, or tenseness and discomfort in the stomach during moments of fear? And yet these sensations are not emotions—they are merely the *reaction* of the physical body to a strong emotional impact.

Nor are emotions a kind of mental activity or energy. Although many of us do confuse our thoughts with our emotions, they are *not* the same. Quite the contrary, they are two completely separate levels of activity. Emotions are designed for use in expressing our attitudes, our humanity, and our love. Thoughts are intended to be used for observing the world, for drawing conclusions, and for focusing convictions.

Still, they are frequently mistaken for one another. Very emotional people attempt to use their feelings when they should be thinking rationally—in making political decisions, in purchasing material goods, in participating in religious worship, in evaluating their own accomplishments, and so on. The majority of voters do not cast their ballots on the basis of clear, rational analysis of the issues; they vote on the basis of emotional appeals, ethnic prejudices, and charisma. Just so, consumers seldom buy items because they need them—they buy because the product looks good, or because they are depressed and need cheering up, or because the sales pitch has struck an emotional chord. And, most churchgoers accept their faith not because they have rationally concluded that its creed is true and helpful, but because they have an emotional need to believe *something*, or because they fear they will perish eternally in hell if they do not.

On the other hand, there are people who regularly attempt to use thoughts when they should be using emotions. These are typically very intellectual people who mistakenly operate on the assumption that it is possible to build a good and caring relationship on thoughts of love alone. Unfortunately, cold and aloof thoughts of love are no substitute for a warm feeling of affection, tenderness, and compassion.

The tendency to confuse thoughts with emotions is more widespread than many of us recognize. It is common, for example, to speak of "mental illness," even if we are referring to emotional disturbances. Moreover, when most of us are asked what we *think* about a subject, we usually respond with our *feelings*–or our likes and dislikes, our prejudices and wishes. As long as we blur the distinctions between thoughts and emotions in these ways, it will be difficult to know when we are dealing with emotions.

Some people believe that emotions are just psychological abstractions; others believe they are the result of muscle tension. Neither of these concepts, however, captures the real essence of emotions.

Emotions are a type of subtle, invisible energy, much like electricity or light, although different in quality. The easiest way to visualize them (since we cannot physically see them) is as streams of living energy that circulate throughout the planet. This emotional energy is alive, active, and has specific characteristics of shape, size, and color. As a living force, it exists independently of human beings, but of course we are influenced by it, conscious of it, and able to use it. Other life forms on the planet use emotional energy, too: dogs, for example, are quite responsive to affection and expressive of devotion and loyalty. Plant life is responsive to kindness, love, and gentleness and grows more rapidly in a positive emotional environment.

Together, these living streams of emotional energy form a vast "sea" of emotions that permeates the entire planet. Wherever we go, this sea of emotions is present and we interact with it. Literally, this sea of emotions is the collective emotional consciousness of all life forms on the planet. Esoterically, it is labeled the "emotional plane" or the "astral plane."

Within the astral plane, there are many grades and types of emotions, all of which can be contacted by human beings—for better or for worse. There are positive emotions, which are based on the qualities of love, joy, strength, and peace. Examples of these emotional qualities include affection, goodwill, tolerance, generosity, benevolence, serenity, reverence, poise, devotion, sympathy, courage, compassion, and cheerfulness. All of these emotions are composed of relatively pure energy and are pleasant to contact. Moreover, they contain healing and revitalizing potencies; they are inherently constructive energies.

At the lower end of the scale are negative emotions. Some of these are selfish distortions or misuses of love, joy, strength, and peace. When love is distorted by the selfishness of possessiveness, for example, it becomes the negative emotions of jealousy, self-pity, grief, greed, or lust. Aspiration that is distorted becomes envy or fear. Other negative emotions, however, are the opposites of love, joy, strength, and peace. These include malice, intolerance, hostility, anger, doubt, disrespect, guilt, harshness, cruelty, coldness, stubbornness, aloofness, anxiety, and melancholy. These negative emotions are composed of coarse astral energies and are distinctly unpleasant to feel. By their very nature they cause disturbances and induce chaos.

Emotions are not just characterized by quality, however; they are also character- ized by intensity. In this regard they are somewhat analogous to the various colors in the spectrum of light. Each color has not only its basic definition, but also many subtle variations of shade, tint, hue, satu- ration, and opacity. There are, for exam- ple, many different shades of red—some quite pale, others vivid; some saturated, others washed out. Bright scarlet and pas- tel pink are both reds, but each has its own distinctive impact on the eye. Just so, there are subtle variations of intensity among emotions. Both embarrassment and mal- ice are negative emotions, but they obvi- ously differ in intensity. Even in its most severe form, embarrassment is relatively mild when compared with malice, which seeks to destroy life. Similarly, the respect one person may have for politeness and good taste may be quite pale next to the intense awe someone else may have for the nobility and greatness of a heroic deed.

These degrees of intensity are produced by our own *interaction* with emotional energy. The strength of our love for another person will depend on how much we direct our emotions toward caring about that individual. It could be a very insubstantial love, which wanes with the first crisis, or a more durable love, which tolerates, supports, and enriches. Similarly, the force of a particular dislike will depend on how fanatically we react to encounters with the object that offends us.

It can be most interesting to examine how much the impact of emotions depends on these reactions to life. Pure emotional qualities such as goodwill, serenity, and affection exist independently of us—they are integral parts of the ebb and flow of the astral plane. As such, they inherently possess great intensity. Yet only by using these positive qualities in our daily life is it possible to increase their potency within our personal consciousness and environment. And so, the cultivation of such positive qualities depends in part upon our individual initiative to express them.

Our negative emotions, on the other hand, are entirely the result of our reactions to life. *Negativity is not inherent in abstract emotional states.* It is produced by our misuse of emotions—our selfishness, our malice, our fear, and our fanaticism.

Due to the importance of this phenomenon of interaction, it will be helpful to distinguish between our *emotional equipment* and our *emotional resources.* Our emotional equipment is the mechanism of consciousness we use to perceive emotions and express them. It can be thought of as our personal collection of emotional qualities, organized as habits, attitudes, and traits—a collection based largely on our memories of earlier emotional reactions to experience. This equipment is composed of a conscious portion and a subconscious portion. Esoterically, it is known as the "astral body" or the "emotional body." By contrast, our emotional resources are the energies we are capable of contacting on the astral plane. The quality of these energies is directly proportional to the quality of our equipment.

If, for example, our emotional equipment has been misused throughout life, in repeated instances of expressing hate, selfishness, pettiness, or contempt, then that abuse will definitely color the kind of emotional resources we can contact and use. In such a case, even if we happened to contact a pure stream of love, our distorted emotional equipment would taint it with negativity and corrupt its quality. This is the reason why, when a hateful person meets a truly loving individual, the hateful individual is not capable of perceiving the love pouring forth from the other. He feels the love, of course, but perverts it by his negative reactiveness. He also feels the intensity of the love, but mistakes it for an intense amount of negativity. As a result, he views the love of this person as arrogance, hostility, or even evil—or in cases where he does recognize it as love, he darkly assumes that the loving individual is just being nice as a devious means of gaining some selfish goal. It is the only motive he knows.

By contrast, if our emotional equipment has been properly attuned to noble expressions, we will be able to use it to contact emotional resources which will raise the quality of our life and nurture our growth—resources such as goodwill, faith, peace, love, and courage. Attuning the emotional equipment in this way requires more than just the intention to be a decent person, however. It requires genuine self-control and cultivation of tolerance, poise, balance, fairness, compassion, dignity, and strength in the way we deal with others and interact with life. As emotional resources are contacted by us and integrated into our consciousness, they are often given form— a form appropriate to their quality.

In their purest essence, emotions do not have form—they are living streams of force. But emotional energy can be, and often is, shaped into definite forms. In this way they become easier to manage, as the human personality is accustomed to dealing with concrete and well-defined forms.

We are all familiar with these emotional forms. The images of our dreams every night are made of emotional energy, as are the pictures stored in our memories. When we recall the face of a friend or the image of a landscape scene, we are working with emotional energy, condensed into forms.

The process of working with such images—imagination—is an emotional function, not a mental one. If handled properly, it can become a creative tool for learning to control and wisely use our emotions. Small children, for example, can greatly benefit from an active imagination to help discharge excessively strong emotions such as dislike, acute embarrassment, and feelings of inferiority. But the converse is naturally true as well: if the imagination is not controlled or used purposefully, it can magnify our problems and multiply our distress. Thus, if a child fantasizes being snatched away by a bogey man because he has displeased his parents, he has used his imagination to take a vague, not clearly defined feeling of failure and give it sharp focus, precise definition, and much greater energy.

Whenever we give form to an emotion,

we are making it stronger by giving it definition and focus. This may make it more useful and beneficial, as in the case of imagining specific ways to be more loving and affectionate to our spouse, our children, or our friends. Or, it may make it more harmful, as in the case of a fear or worry. A vague presentiment of fear is a minor problem in comparison with a sharply-etched picture of being assaulted and robbed by a monstrous person. The latter image, made up wholly by our fantasy, will plague us without cease—during the day at unguarded moments, during the hours of sleep in blood curdling nightmares.

The emotional forms we create throughout life are generally preserved within our subconscious. The more frightful ones are usually repressed, but they can be dredged up in dreams or during moments of great emotional excitation. The milder ones float in and out of our awareness seemingly at random, but always in association with something that is happening to us at the time.

In addition, there are virtually unlimited numbers of emotional forms floating about unattached on the astral plane, and these, too, can be contacted by us—and often are. These are the flotsam of eons of human emoting and human imagination. Some are sentimental, some are outrageous; some are religious in character, others are more materialistically inspired. Many of these forms are perceived by us during our dreams, although most of us mistake them for personal dream images and try to interpret them as such—a futile process. Others bombard our emotional senses during the day, influencing the nature of our moods, our attitudes, and our thoughts—even when the images of these emotional forms are not perceived.

It is wise to understand that these forms are made of emotional energy—either our own or someone else's—so we can police our reactions to them and avoid being trapped by them. Emotional forms can be used beneficially—for example, by creating symbolic images that will embody an ideal pattern of behavior, a loving activity, or a desire for self-improvement. But if used unintelligently, we can quickly become overwhelmed and enchanted by their power. In such cases, our fantasies run free, conjuring up mighty illusions of fear, resentment, bitterness, inappropriate enthusiasm, fanatical loyalties, and excessive confidence.

There is also the possibility of self-deception in dealing with these images and astral forms. It is not uncommon for spiritually motivated but inexperienced people to quiet down their perception through some form of meditation and then begin to pick up various thought-forms of emotional energy rising from the deeper levels of the subconscious. Since these individuals are spiritually motivated, these forms are often mystical in nature—the cross, an image of the Christ, or a vision of angels. Many such people immediately overrate the importance of such images, believing them to be direct inspiration from the heaven worlds. Of course, they are just emotional images emerging from slightly deeper levels of consciousness—

images they created themselves or drew from the plane of emotions. Their experience is an emotional one, not a spiritual one. They have beheld the form of their emotions, rather then *experiencing the quality of the emotions, which could indeed be a spiritual happening.* The result is an excited but erroneous evaluation of the importance of the event.

As a basic guideline for working with our emotions, therefore, we should take care not to become too involved with the forms of emotions. We can use the forms, yes, but we should never let them become more important to us than the qualities ensouled in those forms. When we do, it leads to mistakes and illusions. We perceive, for example, the form of affection and believe it to be affection, when it is not. The quality or essence of affection is the real emotion, not the form.

One moment's contact with the quality of any emotion, be it affection, peace, goodwill, tenderness, or contentment, is worth ten thousand hours of contemplating even the most "inspiring" emotional form—even the thoughtform of the Christ Himself or the entire heavenly host of angels.

Another important characteristic of emotions is that they are magnetic. Emotional energy will either attract us or repel us, depending upon how our emotional equipment responds. Thus, our emotions link us magnetically with objects, people, and situations of life.

The magnetic nature of our emotions is based on the principle that like attracts like. This is unfailingly true. If we like chocolate ice cream, our emotional desire for chocolate ice cream will tend to attract us to it. Our desire will give us motivation to seek out chocolate ice cream, to remove all barriers between us and chocolate ice cream, and to consume chocolate ice cream.

Someone else, however, may dislike chocolate ice cream. Perhaps he fears it will give him pimples, and he is emotionally incapable of handling pimples. In this case, the magnetic nature of his emotions would repel chocolate ice cream, but it would simultaneously attract other related emotions—primarily, other fears. He would develop a fear of other foods, a fear of being ugly, a fear of being fat, and so on. As a result, his fears would magnetically increase in magnitude. He would develop a fear consciousness—and in all likelihood, a pimple complex, too.

Because of the magnetic nature of emotions, they tend to accumulate. Any given emotion will attract to it similar energies from the vast sea of emotions in which we constantly live, and thereby build in strength. Over a long period of years, the emotional buildup of any habit, trait, or attitude can become quite significant. In the case of a positive emotion, such as affection, the aggregation of energy and potency can be a powerful blessing. But the accumulation of negative traits, such as bitterness, jealousy, or fear, can be a terrible curse. Such attitudes and habits poison our consciousness and make us miserable.

As emotions pile up in this fashion, they begin to saturate and distort our perceptions. In short, they act hypnotically— we become dazed and entranced by their power. If uncontrolled, this can lead to fanaticism and emotional intoxication. The bitter person becomes addicted to bitter- ness and would not be "happy" without the tonic of his gall. The selfish individual becomes drunk with self-centeredness and begins to believe that all the world was created either to annoy him or to give him satisfaction. The seeker of pleasure be- comes giddy with his lust for sensation. As the self-hypnotic trance deepens, all other considerations—such as the needs and as- pirations of others—suffer.

Despair and depression poignantly il- lustrate the hypnotic nature of emotions. One uncontrolled moment of despair mag- netically attracts others and soon a habit of depression—a downward spiral of nega- tivity, really—becomes firmly entrenched. When this occurs, even trivial events will trigger long periods of despair. We have hypnotized ourself into responding to even pleasant circumstances with moods of de- pression. Having crowded out the more humanistic responses to life—hope, aspiration, and good cheer—despair becomes virtually the only emotion in our equipment.

Of course, such hypnotic patterns of behavior can be halted and reversed; negativity can be cleaned out and more positive emotions cultivated. But it is a long process involving much hard work, and it can only be accomplished with a thorough understanding of the true nature and purpose of the emotions.

Still another characteristic of emotions is that they are plastic by nature—they lack stability. They are not constant; they are volatile and changeable. In simple terms, they are fickle and—highly unstable. Emotions can have the appearance of a form, for example, but moments later dissolve and reappear in a different form—or disappear entirely. This instability is an important element in the consideration of emotions. As has been stated, emotions are force, not form. While they sometimes appear as forms, the forms are temporary and *always an illusion*. The form appearance of emotions lies in our perception of them, not in their innate characteristics.

This lack of constancy in emotions may come as a shock to the millions of us who seek security in our emotions, who seek stability through our feelings. Emotions are always changing. There is no security inherent in them, no stability. Indeed, the effort to find stability through emotions will always lead to insecurity, frustration, and self-pity. It is like building a house on a foundation of sand: it will be quickly blown away. Thus, if we wish to build a true sense of stability in our life, we must build on a foundation of rock: the rock of our fundamental will-to-be. To find stability of lifestyle, stability of self-identity, or even the stability of security, we must cultivate a solid core of *inner convictions.* These convictions, built in the mind, are based on a commitment to certain carefully chosen ideals and must be a reflection of our basic will-to-be. Only the mind is suited for this work: the emotions are not.

Because emotions are living streams of force, they are inherently active. They do not stand still; they are always in motion. Sometimes this innate activity of emotions is directed and focused; at other times it is not. When not specifically directed, emotions just tend to float about, being attracted to anything or anyone that strikes a responsive chord. In this state, they induce quiet moods or vague feelings. In a pleasant environment, the "free floating" emotional energy will usually form a mood of contentment or tranquillity. This mood will help us relax and set us at ease. In other circumstances, however, the moods will be more negative—a vague state of anxiety, sadness, or hostility that hangs like a cloud over our heads, influencing everything we do and making it more difficult. In this fashion, these lazily floating emotions color our moods and shape the way in which we view the world.

On the other hand, when emotional energy is specifically and purposefully directed, it becomes a most dynamic force that gives us motivation and impels us to act. A specifically directed stream of goodwill, for example, can cause us to extend help to our friends and loved ones, to express generosity, or to engage in constructive activities. Conversely, a focused flow of fear or hostility can impel us to avoid certain people, to make unkind and potentially dangerous statements, and to act in rash ways. These dynamically focused emotions arouse our sleeping energies and activate our desires.

Whether or not emotional energy is moving dynamically or without focus, the important point is that it is always *moving*. It is constantly active, both within the sphere of our own emotional equipment and throughout the entire astral plane itself. Much of this emotional activity occurs on a subconscious level, where we may not be aware of it. Indeed, the flow of emotional energy on the subconscious level often overrides the emotions we are consciously experiencing or expressing at any given moment. For example, we may feel quite content and happy on our conscious level of being, but still be somewhat disturbed by a vaguely defined sense of irritability, fear, or depression on a subconscious level—for no apparent reason.

This kind of disturbance happens most frequently when our subconscious equipment is being influenced either by our environment or by the emotional states of others close to us. Perhaps we are visiting a home where there has been severe disharmony. In such a home, the very walls and furniture will be filled with hostility and bitterness—and our subconscious will sense these negative emotions and be influenced by them. Or, it may happen that we are working quite contentedly at our office, when suddenly we are overwhelmed by a vague but powerful sense of uneasiness. It may only be later that we learn that a family member—miles away from us at the time—was experiencing a substantial amount of anxiety and emotional distress.

Of course, there are also times when we are influenced by our own subconscious memory patterns, not by other people or the environment. We may, for example, be introduced to a new neighbor and dislike him immediately, for no apparent reason. Such a reaction does not necessarily imply that we are psychically picking up negativity from this person on subconscious levels. In all likelihood, the only negativity we are perceiving is welling up from our own subconscious. Some mannerism or facial characteristic of this new neighbor reminds our subconscious of another person in our acquaintance—a person we dislike intensely. The undiscriminating subconscious immediately links the new neighbor with the established dislike, and from then on we regard him with distrust—through no fault of his own.

In this way, we become a negative influence upon our neighbor. Our subconscious begins to disgorge streams of dislike, animosity, and fear, all directed at this person. For his part, our neighbor starts to wonder why he feels so uncomfortable around us. He begins to behave somewhat defensively in reaction, and that only confirms the suspicions of our subconscious, which continues to poison the atmosphere of our neighborly relations. The negativity quickly becomes a downward spiral, affecting us both.

In these few examples, we can see how our personal emotions affect and are affected by the environment in which we dwell and the people we meet. At any given moment, one of two things is happening: either we are polluting our astral environment and are being polluted by it; or, we are lifting up the quality of our environment and are consciously letting the good and noble emotions within it uplift us.

The implications of this statement are serious and deserve careful consideration. Much is made in our modern times of the pollution of our physical environment and its negative impact on the quality of our physical life. The preservation of the physical ecology is important and deserves attention, but unknown to most ecologists, the pollution problem is far worse on the astral plane than on the physical. We human beings often indiscriminately dump the garbage of our emotions, the refuse of our fears and worries, and the contaminants of our negativities into the flowing streams of the astral plane, without the slightest thought of what impact any of it will have on the emotional environment and the others who live in it.

This pollution of the astral environment by humanity has been occurring for hundreds of thousands of years and has become an enormous problem. Often, the environment in which we live emotionally resembles a cesspool of dirt and filth. Of course, no one suffers more than those who do the most polluting, for we each must live in the immediate emotional environment we create. There is no escaping it; if we pour gallons of hate and bucketfuls of malice into the astral environment, that polluted atmosphere will go with us wherever we go, constantly influencing us—for the worse. It will also affect everyone we meet and contact—our loved ones as well as our enemies, those we respect as well as those we hate. Over a long period of time, it will adversely color the quality of our life, for like does attract like. If we habitually pollute the astral plane, we can expect to attract other polluters as friends and associates—until we wallow perpetually in our own noxious fumes and effluence.

The problem of astral pollution can be observed on an individual basis, but it has planetary implications as well. Wherever people gather in groups, a degree of pollution automatically occurs. But in certain areas where fantasy and enmity have freer reign than usual; the problem of pollution increases. A number of cities in the United States, for example, are far more unhealthy to live in emotionally than others. Not surprisingly, these cities are also breeding places for crime, moral bankruptcy, and selfishness. Worldwide, the emotional environments in such trouble spots as Northern Ireland and the Middle East are so polluted and ravaged by hate—and have been for centuries—that any kind of lasting peace faces incredible odds.

Of course, our active use of emotional energy does not have to add to the problem of astral pollution. It will—if we do not exercise control over our emotions. But we do have the choice: instead of polluting, we can choose to use our emotions to lift up the spirits and hearts of others—and to be uplifted ourself.

The key to making this decision lies in understanding that *our emotional sensitivity depends upon the nature and condition of our own subconscious.* If our emotional equipment is purified and wisely directed, we will be sensitive to the energies of love, goodwill, compassion, joy, and serenity. If our emotional equipment is mired in selfishness and negativity, however, then we will be sensitive to the poisons and contaminants of the emotional environment in which we live.

Thus, there is a constant need for self-control and discipline in using our emotions. Emotional energy exists independently of us human beings and has a power and force which is greater and older than we are; emotions can easily overwhelm us and even destroy us if we are not judicious and cautious. On the other hand, like any energy, the emotions can be a most constructive force for expression—when controlled and used with proper intent.

Self-Control

When we make no effort to control our emotions by exerting the discipline of our inner being, they simply follow the path of least resistance. Expression is a natural characteristic of emotions, and they will seek it whether or not they are guided by us. When they are left unguided, however, the results are not usually in our best interests as human beings. Generally, uncontrolled emotions will tend to express themselves in three ways:

1. They will seek stimulation, sensation, and excitement. It does not matter if this stimulation is positive or negative—it is the experience of sensation that attracts the emotional energy. If uncontrolled, the emotions can become virtually addicted to such sensation seeking. They will pour themselves completely into this quest, thus dissipating our strength and leaving us exhausted.

2. They will overemphasize the *wish life* of the personality. Increasingly, we will stop dealing with reality and immerse our-

self in wish fulfillment and fantasy. Rather than face the responsibilities and duties of a challenging but somewhat ordinary life, we will fantasize ourself in unrealistic settings, with unmerited talents and possessions. Or, we may grossly overestimate the value of certain relationships, groups we belong to, or experiences. If indulged in over a long period of time, such fantasy can completely obscure our perception of reality. It bloats the body of our desires and leaves us vulnerable to a wide assortment of fears, suspicions, and unhealthy illusions. It is a form of escape which is decidedly not in our best interest.

3. They will *personalize* our feelings. Rather than seeking to deal with emotions as universal energies, we will become more and more oriented toward dealing with them on a very individualized basis. This leads to narrowness, selfishness, and a lack of objectivity. Our subconscious will not be a storehouse of pure emotional energies such as affection, kindness, and compassion, but rather a picture album of various memories and forms that color all our

emotional perceptions. The emotion of affection, for example, will not be linked with the pure quality of love but rather with a remembered image of some person we are affectionate toward. But there will be other emotions associated with that same image, too—perhaps some resentment or sadness or even grief. As a result, our emotional perceptions and expressions become blurred: we cannot express affection without also getting bogged down in a certain degree of resentment, sadness, or grief. In addition, these personalized associations that we have attached to our emotions get in the way of our thinking and interfere with our objectivity. They introduce errors in judgment and muddle our clarity and comprehension. They likewise open us to manipulation by other people who learn to play upon the inconsistencies and confusion of our emotional patterns.

All three of these forms of uncontrolled emotion contribute to the pollution and poisoning of the astral plane—our emotional environment. And so, there is great need for all of us to increase our control over the emotional energy we use. It helps us and helps the ecology of the astral plane, by cleaning up some of the emotional smog of the planet.

The secret to controlling our emotions is not a very abstruse one. It can easily be understood and put into practice—if we are willing to devote the necessary time and effort and make the required commitment. It involves three steps: first, examining the content of our subconscious and determining where we need to exert more control; second, purifying our emotional equipment so that it is no longer crippled by the effects of negativity; and third, developing a will to find our true self-identity.

The step of examining our subconscious is important because many of our uncontrolled emotional patterns lie buried below the surface of our conscious awareness. We tend to repress the more severe fears, guilt feelings, embarrassments, and hostilities, because they are so unpleasant to think about. But repressing these feelings does not get rid of them or lessen their destructive impact—they continue magnetically to attract to us similar astral conditions. Buried feelings of guilt, for example, will tend to generate a guilty conscience and draw forth similar streams of guilt from other people—strangers we sit next to on the bus or meet in the store, friends we may be talking with on the phone, and so on. Our attraction for guilt will be so powerful that we will even tune in to the kinds of programs on television which will accentuate our remorse. These influences may also unconsciously direct us into behavior that embarrasses us or symbolically punishes us.

Thus, the only effective way to control our emotions is to begin by appraising them objectively and discovering what we must work on. This first step may be somewhat painful if we have been submerged in negativity for awhile, but it will establish a pattern for taking a more active interest in the affairs of our emotions.

Having determined which emotional patterns need disciplining, the next step is to purify them. This process demands patience and the willingness to work over a long period of time, as even the faintest residue of negativity and selfishness must be removed before purification is completed. The most important part of the work of purification is the replacement of negative attitudes, moods, and traits with positive ones—with positive qualities of love, gentleness, kindness, peace, compassion, and cheerfulness. But there are a number of activities which can nicely complement this basic work. The Catholic practice of confession can be helpful in the work of purification, for example, as can the sacrament of communion (in any church). The use of the psychological procedures of forgiveness and blessing are also most beneficial (forgiveness is described later in this book; blessing is described in *The Art of Living: Volume I*).

But purification of the emotions, as important as it is, is *not* enough. By itself, it might lead just to infantilism—a state of naivete and simple-mindedness where everything is nice but not necessarily mature

or constructive. Consequently, it is important to combine the work of purification
with the development of a well-defined
self-image as a competent journeyman in
the art of living. The purpose of such a
self-image is to provide a center of stability
for our emotions. Only when the emotions
are focused in this way can we be sure we
will not lose control.

The best way to create a stable self-image
is by defining the kind of person we want
to be, thereby building a core of commitments, ideals, and convictions we can stand
by. As much as possible, the contents of
this core should be patterned after the
ideal self-image of the soul. The soul is the
part of our being which is ultimately responsible for our life and achievements; as
such, it is the best source for determining
our attitudes and behavior. Letting ourself
be led by other sources—for example, the
dark moods and cravings of the personality—can be fraught with peril. A self-
image based on selfishness or fear will
lower the quality of our life and eventually
destroy us. But the soul has an enlight-

ened view of the kind of person it wants us to be.

Guided by the soul, we can then make fundamental decisions affecting our moods, attitudes, and self-image. We can decide to be cheerful and optimistic rather than grumpy and cynical, knowing that greater stability of consciousness lies in expressing the joy of the soul. We can choose to be forgiving and cooperative in dealing with others, rather than hostile and selfish, realizing that this is the true attitude of the soul. We can elect to act with dignity, courage, and maturity as we confront our daily experiences, rather than worry, fear, and stress.

As we make these choices, we create a set of convictions which gradually brings our emotional expression under control. We begin acting with a plan and with purpose; we infuse meaning into our life.

And we discover the true value of the emotions.

Touching

Some people, of course, resent the idea of controlling their emotions; they prefer to let the emotions control them. But this is not a healthy way to approach the art of living; it distorts and undermines the purpose of the emotions. To deal wisely with emotions, we must understand and cooperate with their intended function—not rebel against it.

More than anything else, emotions are an *energy of expression.* Ideally, they should be used to express the qualities of the innermost self—to express goodwill, forgiveness, affection, tenderness, courage, serenity, tolerance, compassion, idealism, and devotion. When our emotions are used in these noble ways, they relate our individuality to the universe at large—to other people and to our own responsibilities. In this manner, they form a channel which gives focus and expression to the will and intentions of our higher self, the soul. This will and inner purpose have always existed and always shall, but it is through our emotions that we help them manifest on the level of the personality— by clothing them with faith, hope, dignity, supportiveness, enthusiasm, gentleness, concern, and loyalty to inspired causes.

Thus, the emotions serve the purpose of what is called "selfing" by J. Sig Paulson in a remarkable book titled *Your Power To Be.* "Selfing" is the process of manifesting the will of the inner being through the form of the personality. As Paulson puts it, "Through the process of 'selfing' the invisible becomes visible, light becomes form, God becomes man, the Father gives all that he has to and through the Son." The emotions are designed to play a significant role in this process, by focusing the infinite and universal energies of love, joy, and peace into finite expressions of tenderness, sympathy, goodwill, tranquillity, strength of heart, contentment, and good cheer. In other words, they are to be used in specific acts of generosity, healing, succor, and kindness. It is not enough just to bask in vague, general love for all of humanity. After all, it is not love but *loving work* that changes the world and fulfills our purpose.

But even when our emotions are not used ideally, they are still energies of expression. In such cases, they become expressions of envy, malice, possessiveness, intolerance, fear, fanaticism, hate, harshness, unkindness, and selfishness. They are less than desirable and get us into all sorts of trouble, but they are still expressions.

The basic purpose of emotions is to express. It is the nature of emotional energy to behave in this fashion, and whether the expressions are noble or vulgar, it does express! Moreover, from this basic postulate we can draw an important conclusion: any time the emotions are used for some purpose other than expression, that will be an incorrect use.

Sadly, most human emotions are incorrectly used. Instead of being based on the principle of expression, they are used as a sensory device. They are used to perceive what is going on in the world and to draw conclusions about those events. They are used for reacting rather than for expression. For example, we use emotions to gauge our feelings of well-being. Some days we feel sad, other days we are happy. In each case, we are using our emotions as a sensory tool—as a barometer of life. Such usage is a mistake; if we wish to perceive the events of the world and make conclusions about them, we should use our mind. This is the tool that was designed for perception and observation, not the emotions!

To put this idea in another way, it could be said that the emotions should be used for *touching*—for touching others and our environment with the qualities of the inner being. Our emotions are the ideal vehicle for touching others to heal conflict and negativity; for touching others so that they will aspire to the nobility within themselves; and for touching others with the quality of the inner life, so that the humanity within them will be nurtured and grow. In fact, the word "touch" is sometimes used in the context of emotions. We talk of being "deeply touched" by the kindness or generosity of another person. In its fullness, however, it should symbolize the spirit of touching others and lifting up their consciousness to a higher level.

When the emotions are incorrectly used, they become examples of *feeling,* instead of touching. Whereas the word "touching" embodies the concept of expression, the word "feeling" does not. "Feeling" is the use of the emotions as a sensory device—not as a vehicle for expression. To be sure, the word "feeling" is used almost interchangeably with the word "emotions," but that only indicates how widespread the misuse of our emotions is. We use our emotions to detemine how we feel, to measure if an experience or idea feels right—indeed, to feel and grope our way throughout life. Such misuse of our emotions ultimately ends in confusion and misery.

By implication, touching is outgoing. It is the process of using the strength and goodness of our soul to help and uplift others. Feeling, by contrast, is receptive and selfish. It is based on what others can do for our personal ego.

Selfishness suffocates. We become so concerned about what we *want*–both what we want to obtain and what we want to avoid–that the magnetic power of our desires and fears virtually drowns out our essential humanity. As our obsession with possessing objects, people, comfort, and recognition increases, the feeling nature of selfishness becomes so stimulated that we almost lose contact with the rest of humanity, on both an individual and a collective basis. We become so devoted to attending to our selfish wants that we pay no heed to the needs of others, the needs of humanity, or the needs of the universe.

Touching implies that we are in contact with our inner being and can draw upon its resources in order to touch others with them. Feeling, however, implies control by the personal ego with its overemphasis on forms, not qualities; on appearances, not substance. Thus, when we use our emotions for feeling, we are seeking only the *appearance* of wealth, comfort, and status, not the *qualities* of compassion, peace, and wisdom. We cultivate a taste for beautiful possessions and superficially beautiful friends, but we do not cultivate a beautiful consciousness or the genuine qualities of friendship. Because we are only interested in feeling the surface of life, our life ends up empty.

The "feeling" approach to emotions also commonly leads to the perpetual quest for some kind of ultimate sensation—which of course does not exist. In many cases, it does not really matter whether the sensation is pleasant or painful, as long as it is strong. And so, we witness people seeking "ultimate sensations" through sex, through drinking, through drug experiences and self-induced hallucinations, through violence, and by undergoing great physical danger for a momentary thrill. The emphasis is always placed on the thrill and sensation that will be obtained—the "high," to use popular parlance.

The constant quest for such sensations leads quickly to a state of emotional exhaustion and numbness from which it is difficult to recover. It becomes progressively harder to find bigger and better thrills; the appetite for sensation is *never* satisfied. The impossible quest becomes intoxicating and leads to drunkenness of consciousness. The individual's emotional energies are dissipated—spent on foolish activities rather than invested in the purposes of the inner self.

Sometimes this quest for sensation is purely vicarious, but the effect is the same. A classic example of this use of feeling is the housewife who becomes immersed in soap operas until she cannot separate fact from fantasy. Carried to an extreme, she will actually develop a "soap opera consciousness" and be capable of thinking about life only in terms of these television melodramas. This, too, is just an escape from life that leads to emotional exhaustion and makes it impossible for the individual to operate in a healthy and stable way emotionally.

So, instead of using emotions for feeling, we should use them for touching—for expressing the will of the soul in practical ways in our daily life. Selfish people will undoubtedly reject this notion on the grounds that it would force them to share their livingness with others. But this is a foolish, self-deceptive notion, for it is the *selfish* use of feeling that induces emotional exhaustion. Selfishness, the quest for sensation, and fantasy all dissipate our natural energies. These same activities also tend to disconnect us from the sustaining life of our inner being. Touching, on the other hand, does not. Sharing, healing, and aspiring actually replenish our energies, because these acts of humanity establish us as effective channels connected with the rest of the universe. As we serve that universe, it also serves us.

Therefore, using our emotions properly—for the purpose for which they were designed—is no more difficult than using them to touch other people: to touch them with gentleness, with compassion, with serenity, with joy, with friendliness, and with hope. As we do, we lift up their eyes and hearts and give them new faith, new desire. And in this way we individualize our innate goodwill and joy and give it form in our daily life.

Love Without End

Once we have understood the nature and purpose of our emotions, there is only one other step in learning to work effectively with them: we must use our emotional energies in practical ways to fulfill their purpose. Little is gained by mere intellectual understanding; our knowledge must be expressed.

To be successful in this endeavor, we must become familiar with and learn to contact the *living essence* of our emotions. We do not grow emotionally by just manipulating the old patterns of our anger, fear, or worries; instead, we grow by exercising and strengthening the noble components of our emotions. Nor do we grow by trying to substitute thoughts for emotions—a common error in the practice of positive thinking. It would be unproductive, for example, to try to touch someone with the *idea* of affection—only the living presence of affection can have any real impact. Therefore, we must learn to contact the "living presence." This is done by making repeated attempts to express the love of the soul in practical and meaning-ful ways to the people we care about. We can touch the pure essence of affection—or any emotion—only by learning to touch the lives of others with it first.

Developing better emotional expres-sion is not an abstract subject for philoso-phers—it is a practical matter that requires our active participation. The proving ground of purposeful emotional expres-sion is our own daily life—our relationships with other people, our reactions to events, our attitudes in general, and the patterns of our behavior. It is here that we must seek to fulfill the purposes of emotions in our life.

Naturally, we must always strive to use this energy with maturity and a sense of responsibility. It is not only a waste of time but also a literal waste of energy to engage in silliness and fantasy. *Only the effort to express our humanity will actually bring per-manent improvements.* This point can best be understood by illustrating the correct use of emotions.

One of the most common distortions of emotions is fear. Since fear is negative in nature, it is obviously an incorrect use of emotional energy. It is a selfish feeling, based on spending too much time being concerned about some possible personal loss or injury. It is a type of hatred which is especially attractive to many people, as it is usually sanctioned by society. Most fears, after all, draw forth sympathy from our friends, who do not realize that the fear is often just a thin disguise for deeper feelings of hatred and rejection.

Like all negative emotions, fear feeds itself. It focuses so much attention on the hated object that it actually attracts the conditions in which the feared loss can occur. A fear of being embarrassed in front of our peers, for example, will often cause us to withdraw gradually from the company of our friends, seeking isolation. This aloofness would then be commented on by our friends, perhaps even ridiculed, and the feared embarrassment becomes a reality.

The first step in correcting the problem

of fear is to defuse its power. This can be accomplished most readily by putting the energy previously expended in fear into constructive activities. If we fear material losses, for example, we should invest the energy of our fear in constructive activities to earn money. If we fear illness, we should put the energy of our fear into the active cultivation of good health. If we fear the criticism of another person, we should put the energy of our fear into doing things for that person that will cause him to praise us. If we fear losing our talents and abilities, we should put our energy into developing our talents even more and using them in ways that benefit mankind.

Such constructive activity will do much to neutralize the power of fear. It redirects our use of emotional energy, so it can be used for touching others, rather than feeling the possibility of loss. But there is even more that we can do to break this pattern of fear: we can develop an abiding trust in the supportive and protective nature of universal life. Fear disappears entirely when we learn to rely upon the strength and courage and power of Life Itself. Nor is this protection and support imaginary—it is available to each of us through the channel of our own soul. And so, we must learn to trust in life. As we do, we come to see our former fears as the silly things they are, and we *build up* in our personality an immunity to fear.

Another classic emotional pattern is bitterness. Bitterness is a feeling caused by the selfishness of self-pity and a strong dose of intolerance. It poisons the emotional environment we live in—and hurts no one quite as much as ourself. If we are bitter about the nature of our life's destiny, for example, that bitterness does nothing to change the pattern of our life—it simply strangles us slowly as we cut ourself off from the goodness within that destiny.

To transmute this incorrect use of emotional energy into a proper one, we must begin by repairing the damage caused by our bitterness. In other words, we must learn to be forgiving and cultivate an attitude of thankfulness. If we are bitter toward another person, we must forgive him for his misdeeds—and we must seek his forgiveness for our bitterness. We must also strive to become truly thankful for every aspect of our life—even the hardships and miseries that have made us bitter—because only through thankfulness can we begin to perceive the goodness and purpose we have missed all these years. Bitterness, after all, is a terrible blindness; it is an illusion which clouds our perception of goodness. It can only be cured by nurturing an appreciative disposition.

These two examples of working correctly with emotional energy contain the clues for working effectively in transmuting any negative emotion into a positive one: first, the energy of the negativity must be neutralized and defused, not only by eliminating our negative behavior but even more importantly by replacing that negative behavior with a positive, loving, and constructive form of activity. Then, as the discipline of our more constructive behavior takes hold (which may require months or even years of diligent self-control), we likewise must cultivate a greater appreciation for the ultimate purposes of our soul.

It must be emphasized, however, that very little can be achieved unless our intent in making improvements is sincere. Before any genuine changes can occur, we must make a real commitment to be caring and sharing, to nurture a generous heart, and to live up to our responsibilities in life.

There will be times, of course, when we will not be able to live up to our intended behavior. This will cause disappointment and frustration, but if we do not let these emotional reactions overpower us, we can use them to push us along—until we achieve a better emotional expression. What we must guard against is not so much an occasional moment of failure, but rather the attitudes of selfishness, insensitivity, malice, and lack of dedication. We must always strive for the ideal, but if we fall short, we must be ready to cherish and value the partial improvements we have achieved.

Having cultivated this kind of lasting dedication to our own humanistic expression, then it is possible to use the procedures outlined in this essay to eventually master the emotional environment in which we live. And once we achieve this mastery, we are no longer subject to the influence of negative emotions. Because we have built up a high degree of immunity to depression, sadness, grief, anxiety, and fear, they can no longer harm us. In their place, we express love, joy, and a sense of purpose—to everyone we meet.

The key to achieving this mastery of the astral plane, however, lies in mastering our own emotional equipment first. For as we learn genuine self-control, we simultaneously learn to work harmoniously and effectively with the emotional patterns of other people, both individually and collectively. We also learn to contact the pure streams of emotional energy, rather than the diluted energies that most of us live in from day to day.

We taste the pure energy of affection and learn to use it to share in unfettered and unselfish fellowship with others.

We drink of the pure energy of goodwill and learn to use it to nurture the hopes and aspirations within our fellow man.

We are touched by the pure energy of gentleness and learn to use it for touching others.

We are anointed with the pure energy of reverence for all life and learn to radiate this quality to others.

We share in the pure energy of good cheer, for it can only be known through sharing with others.

Ultimately, we discover that all of these pure streams of living energy flow from one fountainhead, from one source, and that they are One. In spite of the wide range and variety of personal emotions, there is in truth just One. There are many expressions, but only one essence—one emotion that encompasses all of life, fills the innermost heart of all, and guides all of life through unfoldment and evolution.

This one emotion is continuous *compassion:* the unfailing love that Christ touched our lives with two thousand years ago; the compassion which He gave without reservation to all alike—to His disciples, to the hypocrites He denounced, to the masses

on the mountain, to the crowds in Jerusa-
lem, to His persecutors on Gethsemane.

Unlimited compassion. Unqualified
compassion. Inexhaustible compassion. It
can be ours, if only we will express it, even
as the Christ expresses it. As He loves us,
so should we love.

As we have *always* been loved, so must
we love now.

Cultivating Tolerance & Forgiveness

A Choice of Weapons

Of all the forms of *ignorance* yet devised by mankind, the most deadly are intolerance and its loyal henchmen: hatred, bitterness, resentment, anger, and vengeance.

Admittedly, the dictionaries do not define intolerance as a type of ignorance. And many people may find it odd to label it as such. We are accustomed to thinking of intolerance as a natural response to something that is wrong, harmful, or different. Indeed, in many cases intolerance seems to be founded on knowledge, not ignorance: the knowledge that someone is attempting to hurt us, the knowledge that someone has made mistakes which irritate us, or the knowledge that someone holds different beliefs than we do. But what seems to be true often is not.

Intolerance thrives on ignorance. It can only exist where ignorance exists. The individual who is intolerant of people with different racial or religious heritages is intolerant only because he or she does not understand that humanity manifests in many forms, all of them at least partially inspired and important. The person who is angered by the behavior of elected officials and curses them with spite and gall has conveniently forgotten that politicians are human beings as well as policy makers and therefore deserve our compassion and pity when they err, as a certain number inevitably will. Just so, the fellow who seeks vengeance after he or his family has been harmed (financially, emotionally, or physically) is tragically ignorant of the order and justice that operate in the universe. And the individual who becomes embittered by the unkind treatment he receives at the hands of others is unwisely focusing on the unpleasant aspects of his life and is ignoring the favors, the opportunities, the help, and the kindness he has also received—possibly from these very same people. In addition, he is ignoring the chance to develop—by responding to the unpleasant treatment in a more humanistic manner—the qualities of strength, maturity, and endurance within himself.

One factor characterizes all these examples. More than anything else, the intolerant person fails to recognize that there are two levels upon which any event in our phenomenal world can be observed and understood: the *actual* and the *ideal.* The "actual" describes the tangible happenings of the event—the fact that so-and-so hurt us, a certain politician has betrayed our trust, or members of a specific religious denomination tend to be rather obnoxious and self-righteous. As long as we are dealing with this realm of the actual, it is fairly easy to be intolerant— even for a person who is highly motivated by the good of mankind. Thus, it is easy to become angry when a politician sponsors a law in his own self-interest, when a criminal repeatedly evades justice, when the "little person" is taken advantage of, and so on. And for the more basely motivated, it is easy to be intolerant in almost unlimited ways: prejudiced against people who are "different," resentful of people who are more successful, or embittered because the universe has not responded to fulfill every personal wish and whim.

The "ideal," on the other hand, is the possibility of perfection in any given situation. At times the ideal is quite visible, as in the kindness or generosity of one person to another. In other instances, the ideal is not visible at all and exists only as a germ of potential. In such cases there are great differences between the actual and the ideal. But no matter how unpleasant, how gruesome, or how destructive the actual events may become, the ideal can always be envisioned by a person who makes the effort to do so.

It is when people ignore the ideal that intolerance is produced. And this is why intolerance is a form of ignorance—and why it is the most deadly of all kinds of ignorance. After all, by ignoring the perception of the ideal in any situation, a person is in effect cutting himself off from similar qualities in his own soul—his inner humanity, benevolence, goodwill, compassion, and kindness.

Many people use intolerance (as well as its byproducts anger, hatred, and bitterness) as a weapon for combating that which they think is wrong in the world. They use it defensively, to prevent further encroachment upon the principles and beliefs they hold dear or sacred. This weapon of intolerance has been wielded by religious institutions, as it was during the Inquisition; it has been used by nations, as it was by Nazi Germany, the Soviet Union, and many others. It is a bludgeon that is frequently used by the self-appointed "underprivileged" in their efforts to restore their "rights"—and by professional merchants of malice, who deliberately stir up the anger of people as a way of inducing change in the world. Intolerance is also employed in personal crusades: to satisfy vengeance; to protect against all manner of feared injuries, real or imagined; and as a means to avoid facing responsibility in troubling situations, such as divorces, personal conflicts, and employment disputes. In short, there are many, many people who obviously believe in the might and the right of the weapon of intolerance.

To use the weapon of intolerance, however, means ignoring the ideal of any situation and descending into a dungeon of ignorance that imprisons the one who uses it. For this is a weapon which backfires and harms no one quite so much as the person pulling the trigger. Intolerant people quickly become bound to a set of reactions that increase in power and magnitude and prevent them from acting affirmatively in their lives. They become trapped in their negative personality traits, totally controlled by whoever comes along and is interested in capitalizing on their pathetic intolerance and ignorance. This ignorance is most devastating in those people who are habitually overwhelmed by resentment, bitterness, and anger. In such individuals, the inner voice of the spirit can be almost completely drowned out by the cacophony of their cursing and spite. Their lifestyle of intolerance can become a *virtual surrender* to the pettiness in other people, to the pettiness in the world, and to the slings and arrows of their seemingly outrageous fortune. The net effect is that they "lose their lives" (they lose their individual capacities for self-expression) to every person that provokes their intolerance: to every incompetent fool, rude person, bigot, and con artist. And to the degree that a person loses his self-expression, he surrenders the ability and opportunity to act in benevolently affirmative and assertive ways which will lead to achievement, productivity, and the capacity to experience peace, joy, good-will, affection, compassion, and wisdom.

The person who makes a habit of using the weapon of intolerance to fight his battles—the angry, rebellious, and unforgiving person so common today—ends up impaling himself on the post of his own negativity. He spends his whole life desperately fighting off the various phantoms of evil that are inevitably attracted by intolerance (because they feed on it). The end result is a pitiful waste of human talent, energy, and time.

Such a person typically believes that the only alternative to his intolerance is passive surrender. He is appalled by the notion of surrender and therefore adopts the opposite extreme—anger.

There is, however, a better weapon than intolerance for "fighting the good fight"—for combating the wrong in the world, in society, and in our individual relationships. It is a weapon that has been proven effective in making permanent improvements in our life; it is effective because it deals not only with the "actual" but also with the "ideal." It is a weapon which harnesses and uses the potent power of the human soul. Consequently, it does not separate and divide, as does intolerance; it unifies and heals. It helps us regain control of our life and our destiny.

This weapon is tolerance; it is applied through a process called forgiveness. It is achieved by shedding our ignorance and expressing goodwill in life.

Tolerance is the automatic result of understanding the fullness of any situation and then acting with dedicated goodwill. The tolerant person observes the actual conditions of life, including all of the unpleasantness involved in them, but is simultaneously aware of the ideal. Consequently, he does not waste any time or energy in reacting to the less-than-desirable conditions of the "actual" with either anger or bitterness, hatred or resentment, vengeance or irritation. Instead, he takes pity on the imperfect conditions of the actual and seeks to reshape them, so they will more perfectly resemble the ideal. If nothing else can be done, at the very least he honors and respects the ideal, which is permanent, as being of more importance than the actual, which is transitory. In so doing, he weakens the force of the unpleasant aspects of the actual and constructively builds greater acceptance in the world for the ideal.

Whereas hatred and anger are the henchmen of intolerance, the servant of tolerance is forgiveness. Forgiveness is the process of applying the ideal to any situation or condition in which the "actual" does not fully measure up to the "ideal." In other words, it is the application of goodwill to unpleasant situations in order to correct them. When a person insults us, for example, we *forgive* him by *forgoing* the intolerant reaction of anger or bitterness we once would have felt. In its place, we respond by honoring the ideal of right speech—the ideal that this person has failed to live up to in his behavior. We do not hold this failure against him, but rather respond with goodwill—in an effort to demonstrate the ideal. Or, when we meet a person who condemns us for having different religious beliefs, we forgive him by forgoing our prejudices and our instincts toward defensiveness and criticism. Instead, we celebrate the common ties of humanity we share with him.

Forgiving is never a matter of *giving in,* as many people seem to believe and fear. It is not a sign of weakness and capitulation. We do not forgive a criminal by indulging him in his criminality or by forgetting his tendencies and exposing our-self unwisely to him. The spirit of forgiveness is in no way incompatible with standing firmly against his criminal behavior—perhaps even using force to stop him, if that is required. Rather, forgiveness involves acting affirmatively with goodwill and compassion to help disabuse the criminal of his antihuman attitudes and actions. Similarly, we do not forgive the anger and malice of another by meekly taking its full blast. We forgive by showing a compassionate willingness to let the past be past and to work cooperatively and constructively together in the future. Nor do we forgive corruption by approving the continuation of that corruption. Instead, we forgive by rooting out the corruption without recrimination, without bitterness, and without endlessly rubbing the offender's nose in the dirt of his or her errors.

To "tolerate" a crime or malicious behavior in the misbelief that indulgence and accommodation are true tolerance and forgiveness is no less ignorant than to respond with hatred, anger, or vengeance.

In both cases, our focus of attention is riveted entirely at the level of the "actual"; we are missing the significance of the "ideal." We are failing to see that there is a difference between what is happening and what *should* be happening, a difference between what is happening and what our reaction to it might be, and a difference between the harmful behavior of another person and his identity as a human being. By failing to make these important distinctions between the actual and the ideal, we blur our perception of what is happening and end up confused. In such confusion, it is possible to make serious errors of judgment—for example, believing that we must surrender to some bigot or criminal.

Nor is forgiveness something that is offered in return for other considerations, although many people do try to use it this way. For example, a family argument may typically end with one of the combatants telling the other: "I will forgive you *if* you will take me out to dinner." Or: "I will forgive you *if* you will never do this again." The implication in such statements is that

the person will go right on hating and being angry with the other if the statement of
contrition or the prescribed penalty is not
forthcoming. In such cases, "tolerance"
and "forgiveness" become signs of approval
rather than signs of understanding an
inner ideal. *Such an abuse of forgiveness is
just as much the result of ignorance as was the
original anger.*

In this particular case, the root of the
ignorance is the belief that charm and
affection can be used to gain advantage
and comfort in life. This is an immature
attitude, but nonetheless one that a vast
number of people still cling to. Such people
use "tolerance" and "forgiveness" on purely
superficial levels, as coin of the realm in
the emotional marketplace of social inter-
course (and counterfeit coin at that). This
false forgiveness has been portrayed hundreds of times in hack movies, as the
central character comes crawling to his or
her lover, begging for forgiveness for having been unfaithful. Only counterfeit forgiveness, however, needs to be begged for.
True forgiveness does not require such

hysterics—it is given with *no strings attached,* freely and without being asked for. Because tolerance and forgiveness are the automatic results of understanding the fullness of any situation, and then acting with dedicated goodwill, they cannot be withheld on a whim, nor do they have to be petitioned. Of course, this concept will undoubtedly be rejected by those people who keep track of every jot and tittle of "goodwill" or "affection" they express. But then, such people express so little of these qualities that it is not hard for them to keep records.

Thus, far from being signs of weakness, tolerance and forgiveness are indications of certain strength. They are emblems of the strength of our innermost being—and the inner ideal. The tolerant and forgiving person demonstrates quite visibly through his behavior that even though the ideal is not being expressed (and perhaps unpleasantness is), he is aware of that ideal and is working with its latent power to hasten its manifestation. He has chosen to work with the weapons of goodwill and compassion and build new and better forms of expression, rather than working with the weapon of ignorant intolerance, which only destroys.

Some people may scoff at this notion that tolerance and forgiveness are signs of strength—that only the tolerant individual is truly strong. These will perhaps be people who have been injured—people who know they have been wronged. They feel that their values and dignity have been violated by the abuses and the prejudices of others, and they cannot accept, as yet, the notion that forgiving those abuses is in any way an indication of strength. Their position is understandable, but is nonetheless grounded in partial ignorance. They mistakenly regard human dignity as some kind of defense mechanism. Thus, if their defenses are threatened, they respond even more defensively.

True dignity, however, is the ability to respond with humanity and goodwill even in the face of destruction and hate. It is exemplified by an instance in Benjamin Franklin's life. As a colonial representative to London from 1757 to 1775, he spoke freely on behalf of his fellow Americans. This activity aroused much ire in England and he came perilously close to being arrested by the crown for treason. As it was, he was subjected to a humiliating experience in which he was forced to stand in a docket called "The Pit" for several hours, while a prosecutor viciously demeaned his "honor" and verbally abused him. If ever a person's tolerance was tested and tried, surely it was Dr. Franklin's during this episode. And yet, when Dr. Franklin was given the opportunity to rebut the charges and clear his name at the end of the prosecutor's tirade, he simply remained silent and strode out of the room. He knew that defending his "honor" and lashing back at intolerance and hatred with anger and self-righteousness would in no way increase his dignity. Indeed, it would only cheapen it. So he chose silence.

Intolerance, hatred, anger, and vengeance are *undignified responses to life.* They devalue human nobility, never enhance it. Tolerance and forgiveness, on the other hand, preserve human dignity and add to its richness and quality, for they are expressions of goodwill and brotherhood. Only the person who has gained the degree of tolerance that Dr. Franklin exhibited in "The Pit" can reasonably hope to maintain his or her dignity in the face of any possible unpleasantness, hatred, or opposition.

There are events which arise in life that are harmful to us and need either to be rejected or strongly disapproved of. And yet the attitude with which we reject these events is of the utmost importance! If we reject danger or harm with hatred, bitterness, scorn, or anger, we escalate the real potential for injury—not lessen it. We risk our dignity, our inner peace, and our mental health. Any expression of intolerance is incompatible with our own peace of mind, our own joy, our own contentment, our own good cheer, and our own goodwill. Therefore, as long as we react to life with hate, bitterness, or anger, it will be impossible to enjoy the fullness of life. We will be sanctioning and contributing to the growth

of an emotional cancer within our psyche—
a cancer that will eat away our inner heritage and consume our dignity.

Still, there may be some people who do
not value their dignity, their mental health,
and their enjoyment of life enough to let
go of their thirst for vengeance, defensiveness, and intolerance. Once they feel that
they have been wronged, they simply will
not rest easy until the wrong has been com-
pensated. They devote their whole lives to
pursuing what they believe to be justice.

To such people it must be stated that
their ability to pursue justice and to rectify
the wrongs they have endured is wholly
inadequate, when compared to the vast
mechanism of balance in the universe.
There *is* order and justice in the universe,
and it works inexorably, without having to
worry about it. It may take some time
before a wrong is fully corrected, perhaps
even a future existence, but the order of
the universe is never violated. And the
universe, being designed to carry out the
cosmic laws of justice, can rectify wrongs
and injuries in far better and more satisfy-

ing ways than even the most scheming, devious, and embittered revenge seeker can contrive. In this universe, no harm can be done to anyone but that it must be repaired and resolved.

Knowing this, we can safely spend our time cultivating the dignity of tolerance and forgiveness. The universe, after all, is on our side—assuming, of course, that we are on its side. And so, if someone has harmed us, we can adopt the forgiving attitude of "leave them to heaven." Why waste time on such people (thus harming ourself even further), when the universe can do the work of balancing and rectifying much more efficiently than we can? Whatever belongs to us will certainly come to us. Whatever others deserve will surely come to them. Just as we do not have to worry about making the molecules in a tub of water move aside to make room for additional molecules when we pour in more water, neither do we have to take a personal role in carrying out justice. The molecules will take care of themselves.

In this context, it bears re-emphasizing

that the attitude of tolerance does not include indulging someone who seeks to take advantage of us, our family, our business, or our property and responsibilities. If we can stop harm from occurring or from doing greater damage, it is our duty to do so. But once harm has been done, it is not our personal responsibility to nurture resentment, bitterness, or vengeance. Instead, the proper attitude is to let the corrective forces of the Sustaining Infinite take over.

Forgiving another person does not mean that he will be freed from the consequences of his or her actions. The universe is never mocked; inevitable consequences are never avoided. Indeed, forgiving in some cases actually allows the wheels of cosmic justice to revolve a bit more rapidly, *as it is a deliberate appeal to the ideal.* Forgiveness helps resolve the problem more quickly. Conversely, a bitter mood of vengeance often *slows down* the natural processes of universal order, because the emotions of anger and hatred magnetically lock up the energies of a situation, impeding justice.

If this is a novel idea, it is only because tolerance and forgiveness have been so widely misunderstood in our ignorance. Tolerance refuses to respond with hatred or bitterness to what others do to us; instead, it responds with goodwill and an understanding of the latent ideal. Forgiveness is the means by which the tolerant person "cleans the deck" of yesterday's arguments, yesterday's grudges, yesterday's injuries, and yesterday's irritation, so he can get on with the vital affairs of today.

This essay, therefore, is an invitation to begin thinking in startling and surprising new ways about life. We must pull ourself out of the trough of intolerance and ignorance and rise up into a higher understanding and perspective. The cultivation of tolerance and forgiveness is not an easy task that can be achieved in an hour or two, or just by deciding that it would be a nice thing to do. It demands honest self-evaluation and a willingness to seek a new revelation—a new revelation about who we are and what we are about. But even more importantly, it requires a willingness to nurture goodwill and express it in our life. For without goodwill and love, we can shatter the blindness of our ignorance and gain greater understanding—but still be just as ignorant and blind as before.

Portrait in Pathos

To fully understand and deal with intolerance, hatred, anger, vengeance, and bitterness, it is necessary to trace these feelings back to their sources—back to their roots. But here is where many people make a major mistake that only intensifies their intolerance and heightens their blindness. The bigot traces his bigotry back to its source and decides that he would not be bigoted if "those people" were not around to annoy him. The angry person traces his anger back to his early childhood and decides that he learned his anger from his mother and father—and so gets angry at them. The hatemonger turns to society in general and places the blame squarely upon the doorstep of all humanity.

Indeed, there are certain types of therapy and "personal development" classes that thrive on helping people find scapegoats for their hate, intolerance, and irritation. Once a suitable scapegoat is fingered, it is then just a question (or so these systems teach) of hating that scapegoat fiercely enough that our hatred will be drained out and we will feel better. Such approaches to therapy are no more mature than the adolescent tradition of burning opposing high school football teams in effigy. No matter what it is called, scapegoat hunting is a primitive exercise more suited for the jungles of Africa than modern civilization. Still, it is surprisingly popular. In some of these systems of therapy, clients are encouraged to pound on walls to vent their anger; in others, they pretend that another client is the object of their intolerance, shouting at him until they feel relieved.

Unfortunately, it is not enough just to vent our negativity; our feelings of the moment are not the roots of our intolerance. (Nor is it intrinsically healthy to dump all our hatred on someone else—

especially a fellow patient who is hateful to begin with.) Accepting these systems of therapy and teaching is tantamount to believing that we could buy an old painting in a junk shop, take it home, clean off all the crusted dirt, oil, goo, and varnish, and find a missing Rembrandt underneath. Most likely, we would just find an empty canvas. It is much the same in life: if we merely work at getting rid of our dirt, underneath we may be left with nothing at all.

The fact of the matter is that the scapegoats we have put the finger on are not the roots of our intolerance. The roots lie *within us*—not in other people or events. They lie in our subconscious patterns of behavior and habit, in the shallow waters of our laziness, our incompetence, our envy, our bigotry, and our irritation. Having made this point, however, it is important to add that these roots which lie within us are *not* inherent elements of our humanity, nor the inevitable fruits of "original sin." Instead, they are the outgrowths of our dealings in life—offshoots of our personal reactions.

Throughout life, we interact with all kinds of experiences—some pleasant, some threatening, some educational, and some of little consequence. None of these experiences makes us either intolerant or wise—but our *reactions* to them do, in time, shape the nature of character. Thus, if we wish to trace the roots of our intolerance, we should begin by evaluating our own reactions to life. Inventing excuses will not help us. It is fundamentally unhealthy to go through life projecting blame—either on others, on God, or on our own destiny. Intolerance begins and ends in our patterns of emotional reactiveness.

An excellent illustration of this idea can be found in the case of the typical "angry young men" (or women) so common today: the rebellious malcontents who stir up dissension in the cause of protecting endangered "rights." Such people would probably try to trace the roots of their self-righteous anger back to parents who did not "love" them enough. But in reality, many of these people are inherently lazy and ill-mannered individuals who merely resented it when their parents insisted that they fulfill a modest amount of responsibility. And when society insists upon the same, they verbalize their resentment and start protesting in the name of protecting their "rights" and "liberties." The real root of their intolerance, therefore, is not the alleged lack of love in their childhood, but only their *own childishness: their refusal to grow up and be responsible.* They are ignorant about what it means to be self-sufficient and productive—and their ignorance inevitably breeds intolerance, dissension, and hatred.

There can be other roots of intolerance, of course, but all of them grow out of our reactiveness to life. Some people, for example, take perverse delight in constantly being critical, argumentative, and faultfinding. They have a sinister lust in their hearts to condemn and degrade. Such hostility is often a cover for their own feelings of inadequacy. They reason that if they can somehow find enough fault in others, they will begin to look pretty good in comparison. And so they carefully nurture intolerance as a defense mechanism.

Then, too, the unfailing principle that "like attracts like" can often be used to uncover other roots of intolerance. In the case of an individual who is intolerant of rude people, it is usually his own rudeness that precipitates the intolerance. The angry individual who objects to the ruthless exploitation of certain groups of people is most likely just trying to clear the field of all competition so he can more easily exploit the exploited himself.

Because they are based on our reactiveness, the roots of our intolerance grow as our immaturity, defensiveness, and paranoia grow. And the more we exercise these reactive patterns, the more intolerant we become. Thus, the more we indulge in anger and hostility, the more we will incite angry reactions from others. Similarly, the more angry others become with us, the more we will become angry with them. Anger will grow and grow within us, until it starts overpowering all other attitudes. Our love, affection, gentleness, and kindness will be blasted out by our anger, for these finer qualities cannot exist in an atmosphere of anger or hatred. The anger will eat away at our personality and corrode our attitudes, until we become a mass of suspiciousness and hatred. Our manners will deteriorate, and we will steadily grow less willing to compromise, less willing to make new friends and try new experiences. We will become an emotional "shut-in," adopting a "you can't win for losing" attitude.

Some people collect stamps as a hobby; others collect stones, matchbooks, or whatever strikes their fancy. The intolerant person becomes a "collector" of injustice, wrath, discrimination, unlikeable people, and pathos. Rather than collect joy, moments of satisfaction and fulfillment, affectionate friends, and enlightening insights, he shuns these in favor of the most negative elements of the human condition.

The long-term consequence of such intolerance is that the individual builds a wall of hatred and resentment to keep the world away. However, this is a prison wall that locks him in more than it locks the world out. It produces loneliness, by cutting him off from all but the most moribund friendships; it strangles productivity and meaningful work. Esoterically, it separates him from his own inner being—from the soul. Thus, the fountain of life is turned off at the source, and the creative potential dries up. While this may seem a bit cruel, it is in truth only a natural part of the order of the universe. If we walk directly into the path of a moving truck and are seriously injured in the ensuing collision, it would be silly for us to believe that the universe was cruel for letting us be hurt. We were injured on our own initiative. Just so, if we damage life by being hateful and intolerant of its manifestations, we damage ourself. Our intolerance blocks off the life forces that would otherwise sustain us and inspire us, and the quality of our life declines. In essence, we are hating life.

More simply put, if we hate God's creations, then we also hate God. And in so doing, we declare a complete bankruptcy of spirit.

Such spiritual and creative bankruptcy is the pathetic consequence of nurturing intolerance and anger as an attitude toward life. When intolerance is sustained for a long period of time, it leads to chronic hostility, argumentativeness, and constant irritability. But more seriously, it eventually produces clinical paranoia, confusion, premature senility, and mental illness as well. The physical body is also affected: intolerance is destructive to the nervous system, the heart, and the gastrointestinal system.

Negativity destroys. But it destroys no one so much as the person who indulges in it, who lives in it, who chooses it as the weapon with which he fights his struggles. "He who lives by the sword dies by the sword." He who ignorantly lashes out with the force of intolerance will be injured by the backlash far more than he was injured by the event or person that induced his reaction of intolerance. He will be buried under a mountain of anger, hatred, and negativity—a mountain of his own making. He will become a portrait in pathos: pathetically paranoid, pathetically ignorant, pathetically petty, pathetically defensive, and pathetically unhappy.

Building Dignity

There is a famous line uttered some years back by the comic strip character Pogo: "We have met the enemy and it is us." In the matter of intolerance, hatred, and bitterness, this is all too true: our enemies are not the people we cannot tolerate. Our enemies are our reactions of resentment, vengeance, and anger. The enemy is us. But we can stop being our own enemy and thus avoid becoming the pathetic victim of intolerance—our own intolerance—described in the forgoing portrait. We can stop being our own enemy and thus stop being victimized by every petty person, every hateful person, and every paranoid that comes along and tries to capitalize on our weakness and emotional addiction. Instead, we can begin to build a more dignified expression—

the dignity of tolerance and forgiveness.

The first step in building tolerance and forgiveness involves cultivating a measure of detachment: we must learn the difference between *who we are* and the anger, hostility, or bitterness we have been expressing. We detach ourself from our intolerance by recognizing that this has been our *behavior*–not our true identity. People have been able to play upon our intolerant behavior and take advantage of us, because we have willingly let our behavior block off and imprison our inner consciousness. But now we do not have to be the whipping boy of our intolerance any longer; we can detach ourself from it and restore the dignity of our inner goodwill. No longer do we have to be sucked into the manipulative games of all the con artists and hatemongers of the world; we can begin to control our reactions.

To gain this first bit of detachment, it is not necessary to actually start liking these other people right away; it is enough just to resolve that we are not going to let them control our reactions anymore. And so we resolve to stop getting angry when others provoke us—just so we can regain control of our life and our dignity. We resolve to stop playing the wounded martyr. If others want to bad-mouth us or criticize us, that is *their* business; *our* business is not to react to their taunts by arguing with them or defensively trying to preserve our "dignity"—which would only cause us to lose it. So, we remember the example of Dr. Franklin and try to live up to it—by being quietly dignified in the face of bitter railing. We learn that we can let the words float by us without hurting us. Moreover, we conclude that we do not have to be right all the time—we do not have to win every argument or get in the last word. Knowing what the true source of our dignity is—the inner wells of tolerance and forgiveness—we can forgo the temptation to resort to counterfeit dignity.

A second aspect of this practice of detachment is realizing that there have been various events which have provoked our intolerance, but these episodes all belong to the past. They do not continue on—except in our continued reactions to them: our continued bitterness, our continued hostility, our continued fear, and our continued thirst for revenge. And so we develop a consciousness that focuses on today and leaves yesterday to bury itself. As Paul put it: "Forgetting those things which are behind, and reaching forth unto those things which are before, I press toward the mark."

So many of us sustain conflicts by living in the past! We remember what a colleague did five years ago, or what our spouse did ten years ago, or what happened to us in the summer of '62. We hold these grudges, and every time we think of the person involved, we associate our unforgotten and unforgiven resentment and anger with him. Specifically, we associate them with his faults and frailties and failures, and thus sustain intolerance.

Today should never be cluttered with the walking ghosts of yesterday. We must update ourself and become a new model person. We would never consider driving a car made with an engine from the 1941 model year, the clutch from the 1945 model, the muffler from 1952, the steering wheel from 1959, the chassis from 1965, and the carburetor from 1973. The various parts would not fit together properly, and worse yet, they would all be out-of-date! We need a new model car with all new model parts. Yet many of us live in the past, perpetuating 1953 model hatreds, 1961 model intolerance, and so on. We need to update ourself and detach ourself from all these things of the past. Then we can become free in the present to express our inner dignity—our tolerance and our forgiveness.

As we untangle ourself from the webs of the past, it is also necessary to detach ourself from the attitude that the other people involved ought to be making changes, too. So many of us put off overcoming our intolerance because we insist that "the other guy" start making some changes, as well as us. And since each person is waiting for the other to begin, the beginning never occurs. We must recognize that the most effective way to change how others treat us is to change how we treat them. The old statement, "Do unto others as you would have them do unto you," has become hackneyed through repetition—but certainly not by application. It is still as relevant as ever. If we treat people badly, we can reasonably expect to be treated badly ourself. But if we treat people kindly and with dignity, we can expect to receive that same consideration in the vast majority of instances.

Of course, it is not just enough to treat people kindly on a superficial level while we go right on hating them deep within. Although most people are not very psychic, they will pick up subconsciously the underlying attitudes that we are constantly broadcasting from our own subconscious. If we are viewing them with contempt, irritation, or hatred, then those inner attitudes are forming our real behavior—not the superficial veneer of politeness and pretense that we are trying to fool them with. The chip on our shoulder may be invisible, but it is psychically palpable nonetheless. As long as it exists, there will be people who will make sport of trying to knock it off. And our intolerance—and ignorance—will continue.

Our effort at gaining detachment can be helped as well by realizing that not all of this intolerance and negativity has been for nought. Out of all this seeming waste, we can nonetheless salvage some meaningful lessons in the art of living. In many cases, having to endure the bitterness or opposition of another person serves to make us stronger and wiser. Sometimes these new strengths and qualities are achieved at a tremendous price of suffering—but these new insights do help offset the losses we have experienced. And by realizing what we have gained, it becomes easier to stop holding fast to our grudges, intolerance, and anger. We do not even have to subscribe to the notion of "sadder but wiser." If we are wiser, why be sad about it? If we are wiser, why remain intolerant? Why continue to lick our wounds and seek revenge? Have we not gained something priceless—wisdom?

We can also consider the idea that we

have, in all likelihood, gotten exactly what we deserved in life. If, for example, we have been nasty to others, and then ourself have been the victim of someone even nastier, we must realize that we were inviting this unpleasantness all along. *Even if we are satisfied with our immaturity, the universe will not put up with it forever.* Sooner or later, the whistle will be blown and a penalty assessed. In such cases, it does no good to curse and swear at the referee. It is much better to accept our fate with dignity—with tolerance.

By considering such avenues of thought, we can gradually diminish our ignorance and build some detachment—the first step toward cultivating tolerance. Then we can go on to the more active work of resolving the conflict involved in any specific situation. In doing this, it is helpful to start by making an inventory of our attitudes and reactions in the specific case.

Note well that this inventory is not a list of all the harm some other person has done us or all the imagined harm society has inflicted upon us. Rather, it is an inventory of our own attitudes and reactions. It is an evaluation of the roots of this intolerance, of our lack of detachment, of our own contributions to the problem, and of all the possible reasons why this situation has developed. And so we consider many questions. What has been our role in what is wrong? How did we aggravate the situation? How have we hurt ourself through our intolerance? What has been caused by our inaction? How have we sustained the unpleasant effects of this experience? How have we invited and permitted others to manipulate us and rob us of our dignity?

Once we have examined the situation in this preliminary way, we are then ready to take the really meaningful inventory—to discover what is right about this situation. We consider, therefore, what is right with the world, what is right about other people (especially the ones we have been intolerant of), and what is right with ourself. What do we value? What can we praise? What are we proud of? What do we stand for? What are our highest and most worthwhile convictions? What do we want to build? What are our goals and commitments? What kind of person do we want to be—once we shake off the shackles of intolerance? How do we want to treat other people? How do we want to present ourself to the world?

There are many questions that must be asked in this inventory; these are just a few suggestions. This is an evaluation of where we stand—and where we want to stand. And as we begin to consider these questions, we start to tap our inner being to a degree—we begin to be guided by our underlying sense of dignity and values. Moreover, this line of questioning gives a new focus to our efforts. Whereas until now we have been dwelling on what we disliked and hated, and thus built walls of intolerance, now we are considering what we can like and what we can approve of. This activity lets us build dignity.

It may take some imagination to find something to praise or like in some situations, especially where real injury has been done. But if we remember that the ideal always exists in every situation, even if it has been grotesquely distorted in the actual circumstances, then we will always be able to find something to approve of—the ideal. If we stop short of finding something to praise, then we are only energizing our intolerance further. We are consigning ourself to the depths of ignorance anew. So we must not let this occur.

It is possible to become tolerant of a con artist who has cheated us of money and caused us embarrassment, for example, by recognizing the skill and talent that was required to con an intelligent person. Someday he will learn to apply his talents in an honest way—this represents the ideal—and so it is possible to forgive him as a fellow human being. Perhaps this very episode, once he has been caught and forced to face justice, will convince him to reform his ways. If not, he will have to undergo additional embarrassment and hardship before he turns his talents to something more constructive. But his talent is something that can be admired.

Our tolerance and forgiveness in such a

case can be heightened even more by realizing the sad stupidity of the con artist. Were he able to apply those same talents in an honest manner, he would be able to acquire far more prestige, wealth, and dignity—and keep them, because he would have acquired them legally. But pathetically, he is so ignorant that he believes he must cheat and deceive people. And so his elaborate scam—which we thought victimized *us*—actually reveals his own ignorance of the workings of the universe; it reveals that *he* is a victim of his own self-deception. Why hate or be intolerant of a person who is that ignorant? His own dishonesty will teach him the value of honesty far, far more poignantly than our anger. Indeed, all that our intolerance will do is blur the issue and make it harder for him to learn his lesson.

An excellent example of intolerance and hatred involves the Watergate affair in this country. Many people who would normally pride themselves on being very tolerant became insane with hatred and rage that they directed at former President

Nixon. They became absolutely ugly with anger at the mere mention of Nixon's name—and still do. And yet Mr. Nixon did not cause their anger and intolerance; their own reactiveness and ignorance caused their hatred.

For these people to overcome their intolerance, they will have to take stock of their reactions and see how they contributed to their anger. Then they will have to consider what was and is *right* and praiseworthy about the Watergate affair and the former President. Surely the deception, the criminal activity, and the cover-up were not right. That can and should be condemned. But it can be condemned with tolerance, with forgiveness, and with goodwill. It does not require the insecurity and pettiness of screaming, cursing, and hating.

In this particular episode of the national life, it is not at all difficult to see that much of value has resulted from the deception itself. Due to Watergate, the country redefined its set of values. What was not considered corruption ten years ago is now considered corrupt. Thus, we have raised the level of moral consciousness in this country to a slightly higher plateau. This improvement is of enormous significance, although most people are too short-sighted and immersed in their intolerance to recognize it. Furthermore, through the Watergate affair the United States was able to demonstrate to the world—and to the world of dictatorships and totalitarians in specific—that a democracy can be shaken and subjected to great pressure and still remain stable. The business of government does not come to a grinding halt but carries on; a peaceful transition can be made and elections continue to be held at regularly scheduled intervals. This, too, is an important benefit of this event and deserves our praise.

It happens that President Nixon and his assorted co-conspirators were caught in the cutting edge of our national growth. That they were caught in their indiscretions is undeniable; that they have suffered for them is obvious. But to hate them and despise them for having been the ones is childish and immature. These are men of enormous talent and capacity; they must be, else they would not have risen to the positions they held. Political leanings aside, they devoted their lives to public service and performed useful work. There is much to praise about them, and therefore we should be tolerant. *This is not a question of making heroes out of them, for heroes they clearly are not.* They have committed errors and are receiving their just deserts. But to ignore their contributions and to descend into the ugliness of hatred and scorn is a totally unreasonable reaction! Through their errors, they have demonstrated that they are human beings with weaknesses and flaws. As such, they deserve our pity and compassion, our forgiveness and good-will—not our vengeance and anger.

Perhaps the greatest revelation in the whole Watergate scandal has been the demonstration of intolerance by such a vast number of Americans. Watergate has brought hatred and anger out into the open and given many of us something to work on—our reactiveness.

In considering the situations of our life, whether they be national events such as Watergate or events at home or at work, we can best cultivate tolerance by taking the attitude that a wise parent would take in dealing with a child. The parent knows that the child will occasionally make mistakes—after all, he is immature and learning. So when the child does err, the wise and loving parent will promptly correct the error and show the child the ideal pattern of behavior, but he will simultaneously forgive the child with affection and compassion. He will not hold a grudge or build up resentment, because he can clearly see that there is a significant difference between the child's behavior and the child himself.

To cultivate tolerance, we must be willing to extend the same forgiveness and goodwill to adults, groups, institutions, and national leaders who may from time to time suffer a lapse of decent behavior—because of their immaturity. In no way does this suggest approving of their behavior, any more than the wise parent approves of the child's indiscretions. Rather, it simply means that we "live and let live"; we accept the other person's humanity.

Even when the other person has not seen the mistake and "repented," we must be tolerant. Being human beings, we are all susceptible to the blindness of ignorance. While a mistake may be clearly obvious to one person (the victim), it may not be at all clear to the person committing the mistake. And so, remembering our own moments of blindness, we must be willing to be tolerant of the other person even when he spurns contrition. To do less is to sustain anger, hatred, and resentment.

The activity of seeking out the praiseworthy and the ideal in any situation is by far the most important work in cultivating tolerance and forgiveness—much more important than making an inventory of our reactions, which is just a preliminary step. It leads to understanding, even though it may be a thorny and difficult route to follow at the start, if we have been mired in our hatreds and dissensions. In pursuing this work, however, we must make sure that we are genuinely building tolerance and dignity and not just shoving our intolerance onto a back burner, where it can continue to simmer and boil.

Many people who believe they have become truly tolerant and benevolent have merely lapsed into apathy and indifference, coldness and aloofness. These are not signs of tolerance—in fact, they are subtle manifestations of intolerance! Apathy and coldness are consorts of the same old bogey man of ignorance. Thus, such people are deceiving themselves and still have much work to do before becoming forgiving people. Typically, they artfully dodge having to face their problems; having removed the objects of their intolerance, they then conclude that they have become tolerant. They believe they have forgiven their brother-in-law, for example, when what they really have done is ignore him. Or, they believe they have mastered their dislike for their former spouse, when what they actually have done is forgotten him or her. Such an approach is like hanging a suit of dirty clothes in the back of the closet, where it is out of sight, and then believing it has been laundered. But when the suit is needed again in the future, the unresolved problem will be rediscovered.

The clues that we are substituting indifference and apathy for true goodwill are easy enough to detect: any mention of the person or situation we were once intolerant of will hit a raw nerve. We will not be able to take a joke about it or laugh at ourself. And there will also be a general lack of joy and grace in our attitudes—because we have not actually built up our dignity. We have built only a wall of aloofness. Such trouble signs indicate buried conflicts that need attention—and soon.

It is for this reason that it is so important to discover what we can like and praise about a situation—to discover the ideal. But it is not just enough to know we *can* like something—we must also do it. We must contact the energy of goodwill and express it in the circumstances and relationships of our life. We must actively begin liking and cherishing—if not the people who have hurt us, then at least the maturity we have gained by living through these events.

We must begin forgiving.

A New Revelation

Once we realize that our hatred and resentment have been victimizing us far more than they have been hurting the person or event we have disliked, it is possible to turn off our anger and irritation and start developing tolerance. In the beginning, however, it is often much more difficult to start actively forgiving. The seeming impossibility of ever being able to forgive should not discourage us from trying to cultivate tolerance. It is enough to start with what we are emotionally ready to attempt and then go on from there, step by little step. It may take months of cultivating detachment before we can face the prospect of actually forgiving, but that should not be a cause for despair. The first consideration is always realizing that our injuries will be adjusted by the universe—

it is not up to us to kill ourself with bitterness, curses, and vengeance. Nor is it very
wise.

Forgiveness becomes possible as we
gradually learn to see the humanity within
the person or situation we have so thor-
oughly despised. And so we must open our
eyes and begin to look with pity at the
pathos of what the other person has tried
to do. A greater measure of pity will help
trigger our buried capacities for forgiveness and acting with goodwill.

Thus, we consider the probability that
this person simply did not know any better. Surely, if he had realized the long-term
consequences of what he has done to us,
he would have behaved quite differently—
and more responsibly. Because he has
acted ignorantly and will suffer for that
stupidity sometime in the future—the order of the universe guarantees it—he does
not deserve our wrath: just our pity.

Similarly, we can spend a moment contemplating what it must be like to live in
the mind and heart of a person such as
this—a person who is so misguided, so em-

bittered, so joyless. It must be pathetic to live trapped in such a shell of cruelty or paranoia or rudeness, to hate the world so much. Yes, he has hurt us, but now we begin to see that *he has to live with his crabbiness, criminality, or irresponsibility twenty-four hours a day!* Not only that, but he also has to live with his unpleasant future. That is something we will not have to undergo—not if we are developing tolerance.

And so, as we begin to recover from feeling hurt by his impositions, we can begin to experience the first real trickle of goodwill and forgiveness by seeing just how pitiful his situation really is. We can sympathize with this pitifulness, because not too long ago we were behaving in a fairly pathetic way ourself—when we were reacting to his anger, his rudeness, his hatred, or whatever it was. We wasted time and energy, too, by maintaining our intolerance and our chip on the shoulder. So, having been there, we can sincerely come to know pity for this person. And as we increase our appreciation for what the underlying ideal of this situation is—the ideal known to our inner being, our soul—that, too, opens wider our capacity for being forgiving.

There is no way we can get a glimpse of the inner ideal of any situation of life except through our own insights. The ideal is an embodiment of our spirit—of our wholeness, our wisdom, our decency, and our spirit of justice. When buried in intolerance, we are inevitably ignorant of these inner strengths. We know only the "actual"—the less than perfect. But as we begin to think with detachment and to act with tolerance, then the light of the ideal can pierce our darkness and illuminate our path. We set aside our need to assess blame, our temptation to strike back, and begin to realize that the truly *strong* person seeks to heal, not destroy. And this healing begins within. Then, as we heal the cancer of our resentment and bitterness, the healing force reaches beyond us, setting an example that will affect the behavior of others. Our own efforts at becoming tolerant will touch others and lift them up, to help them overcome the negativity of their impulses and behavior.

Finally, if we persevere, we will discover that we have the strength within us to *give up* all resentment, bitterness, anger, and intolerance—and that we *want to,* because our dignity and honor are impaired by every negative thought and feeling we express. We will become more aware of our inner spiritual heritage, and choose to be guided by it, rather than our reactiveness.

It is perfectly natural at this stage of self-realization to experience a measure of quiet shame for the mistakes of the past—not a shame that smothers and leads to despair, but a shame which helps us resolve to increase our goodwill. We cannot change the past and must not squander time lamenting what belongs to yesterday, but we certainly can choose a more forgiving and compassionate pathway in the future. And so, just as we have found that we can begin to forgive others, because we have discovered pity in our heart, so also can we now forgive ourself. We can tolerate our weaknesses.

In no way does tolerating our weaknesses mean indulging in them, any more than tolerating a criminal means approving his ill deeds. Forgiving ourself is the same as forgiving anyone else—we forgo the temptation to react with bitterness or hatred when disturbed by our human frailty. We reach out and grasp the ideal and try to apply it to the actual. In this way, we accept ourself, just as we must accept others. We accept the wholeness of our being, just as we must accept the wholeness of life itself. The wholeness of our being includes our weaknesses and uncorrected behavior, as well as our spirit, our dignity, our strengths, and our compassion.

This is true repentance—accepting the wholeness of our being and directing the good within us to overpower and master the imperfect within us. Repentance has nothing to do with going to church and confessing to a priest or minister our sundry "sins." Nor does it have much to do with going to an analyst and regorging all the lurid details of our past. It means becoming aware of the fact that we have made a mistake, and then resolving to use our inner strength and dignity to prevent ever making that same mistake again. Repentance acknowledges our blemishes, but then invokes a change of attitude and heart, so that we become genuinely tolerant of others. Repentance produces a transformation in character and leads to a new revelation *of who we are.*

This new revelation gives us the *strength* to be forgiving—a strength that is rooted in our spirit. With repentance comes an infusion of wisdom into our personality. We begin to see events and other people in a new light, with a greater measure of understanding. This new revelation, which not long ago was only the most fleeting glimpse, grows within us and gives us the resources we need to be forgiving—even if we once considered that to be impossible.

Principally, this is a revelation of our own dignity. But oddly enough, it is revealed to us *indirectly,* by reflection in others. As we start seeing the same dignity of inner humanity within others—especially within those people we have previously been unable to forgive—then our own dignity is revealed to us. Only when we have learned to see latent, unborn saintly qualities in others can we experience the revelation of those same qualities within our own consciousness.

But the revelation is not just one of new wisdom. It is also one of new goodwill and compassion. Seeing that the saintly qualities are still unborn in these other people—because they have not experienced the transformation of this new revelation—we begin to perceive the true pain and suffering they taste. Having seen the ideal, we can now appreciate more fully the wide gap between the ideal and the actual, and the hardship that faces any individual who is still unaware of the ideal—any individual who still dwells in ignorance and intolerance.

When the revelation described in these words becomes our direct experience, and not just promising words on a printed page, then we have started looking on the world and on others as the soul looks, as the soul knows. With our eyes now open, we therefore adopt a new attitude, taking care never to add to the suffering of others by expressing anger or irritation. Rather, we do what we can to soothe and heal and open the eyes of others to the difference between the actual and the ideal. We forgive.

In other words, cultivating tolerance requires the ability to understand life as the soul understands it, and to act as the soul acts. The soul perceives hatred and anger, injury and hurt; the soul does not approve of these imperfections, but it always seeks to heal with love and compassion. It always seeks to render the imperfect more perfect. The soul forgives, and in so doing, nurtures life with its own inherent dignity.

The key to tolerance, therefore, is learning to see and emphasize what is *right* in our life, in other people, and in events. For the light of the soul—the very substance of the new revelation—only sees itself in its own reflection. If it cannot see its dignity, its tolerance, its nobility, its strength, and its goodwill in our attitudes and behavior, then it cannot enlighten our life on the personality level. The light will remain hid, for there will be no compatible elements for it to transform. Sunlight cannot pass through blackened windows, but it can pass through clean ones. To become tolerant, we must establish a "window in consciousness" through which the light of the soul can shine.

The windows of our consciousness are cleaned through forgiveness, for forgiveness is a deliberate act of reaching out and lifting up other people through our own surprising strength and goodwill. As we develop this ability to act as the soul acts, our life is automatically filled with grace, tolerance, and forgiveness.

With this personal revelation also comes a new understanding of how and why we fit in with all people, and this, too, lifts us to a new degree of tolerance. This is the revelation of brotherhood and the need for working in unity with all men and women— not in dissension, hostility, or anger.

It is not easy to write about brotherhood, because the very word is one that
has been seized upon by intolerant people
of many types and distorted into shapes
and sizes very different from its true reality. The concept is often reduced either to
a notion of mere equality, where everyone
is equal in his mediocrity, or to an idea of
solidarity in bigotry. In this era of populist
and communistic prejudices, the lofty ideal
of brotherhood is sadly reduced to the
equivalent of mass gratification.

In its purer sense, brotherhood implies
that there can be a rich variety of differences in the human race—differences of
talent, experience, authority, and compe-
tence—and yet all humanity works together
with a communal spirit of caring and sharing. Each individual works with a sense of
benevolent responsibility and participation—a spirit that is neither patronizing
nor groveling.

This is the ideal of tolerance and forgiveness—and also the goal. Obviously, we
have not yet consummated the goal—but
the ideal is real nonetheless. Of course the

world is imperfect, but it is evolving and improving, and we as individuals can contribute to its unfoldment. With responsibility. With goodwill. With talent. With tolerance. With forgiveness. With brotherhood.

Once we have glimpsed this revelation, we realize that condemning the bad never makes anything better, even though we might wish that it would. Only constructive building improves our lot. To reduce this idea to its simplest possible terms, *only making things better makes them better!* In this tautology lies the heart of tolerance and forgiveness—and the key for cultivating them.